RICHARD MOYLE

POLYNESIAN SOUND-PRODUCING INSTRUMENTS

SHIRE ETHNOGRAPHY

Cover photograph
During their visit to Tonga in 1953, Queen Elizabeth II and the Duke of
Edinburgh were serenaded at dawn by four nose-flute players outside their
bedroom in Queen Salote's palace in Nuku'alofa.
Photograph: Luis Marden. Copyright: National Geographic Society.

British Library Cataloguing in Publication Data:
Moyle, Richard
Polynesian sound-producing instruments.
1. Polynesian musical instruments
I. Title
784.1996
ISBN 0-7478-0095-2

Published by
SHIRE PUBLICATIONS LTD
Cromwell House, Church Street, Princes Risborough,
Buckinghamshire HP17 9AJ, UK.

ISBN 0 7478 0095 2

First published 1990.

Printed in Great Britain by
C. I. Thomas and Sons (Haverfordwest) Ltd,
Press Buildings, Merlins Bridge, Haverfordwest, Dyfed.

Contents

Acknowledgements

I would like to thank the following individuals for permission to publish their field photographs: Ken George, Jenny Little, Ad and Lucia Linkels. I am grateful to the following museums and their staff for permission to publish many of the other photographs: Museum of Mankind, London; University Museum of Archaeology and Anthropology, Cambridge; National Museum of Ireland, Dublin; National Museums of Scotland, Edinburgh; Rijksmuseum voor Volkenkunde, Leiden, Netherlands; Musée de l'Homme, Paris, France; Museum für Völkerkunde, Dresden, Germany; National Museum of Victoria, Melbourne, Australia; Metropolitan Museum of Art, New York; Bishop Museum, Honolulu, Hawaii; National Museum of New Zealand, Wellington; Auckland Institute and Museum, Auckland, New Zealand; Canterbury Museum, Christchurch, New Zealand.

The cover picture is by Luis Marden, *National Geographic Magazine*. Figures 4, 9, 16, 22, 23, 24, 28, 36, 37, 38 and 39 were photographed by Andrée Brett and Maureen Lander. Figure 22 (right) is by Charles Uht. Figures 2, 3, 6, 7, 12, 14 and 33 are by the author. Figure 29 originally appeared in the *Sydney Morning Herald* on 9th June 1976. The map (figure 1) is by Caroline Phillips.

4

List of illustrations

1
Introduction

Within the vastness of the Pacific Ocean three broad cultural regions were identified by navigators and cartographers in the eighteenth and nineteenth centuries (figure 1): Melanesia ('Black Islands'), with the largest and most heavily populated islands, and also the longest history of human habitation; Micronesia ('Small Islands'), with its many low atolls and relatively small population; and Polynesia ('Many Islands'), colonised in a series of broad eastward migrations from the west, and whose cultures and languages are more homogeneous. Around 1940 researchers noted a division of Polynesia itself into Western and Eastern on the basis of culture, and this division remains valid today.

Western Polynesia includes the islands of Tonga, Samoa, Tokelau, Tuvalu, Niue, Uvea and Futuna. (It also includes several isolated islands lying inside the political territories of the Solomon Islands, Tuvalu and Papua New Guinea. These islands, called Polynesian Outliers, were colonised by return westward migration from Western Polynesia after that region itself had been settled and have retained their Polynesian culture despite being located within Melanesia.) The settlement of the region began with Fiji and then, some three thousand years ago, migration to Tonga began, followed by northward movement to the other islands. Fijian culture has long been recognised as transitional between Melanesian and Polynesian. On the basis of present knowledge, Fijian sound-producing instruments appear to have more affinities with Polynesian forms than with typical Melanesian models, and accordingly Fijian specimens are included in this present work. (Because not all the specimens described in this volume are associated with music — some are signalling devices — they are grouped together under the term 'sound-producing' rather than 'musical' instruments.)

The clustering of these island groups and the development of large ocean-going double-canoes permitted two-way voyaging, and contact for the purpose of trade or marriage was common until the mid nineteenth century, particularly among Fiji, Tonga and Samoa. Remnants of this contact still exist in the form of local place and personal names, man-made structures, ceremonial privileges and the retention of the original language among small groups of residents. The musical results of this contact include the spread of several musical instruments, as well as

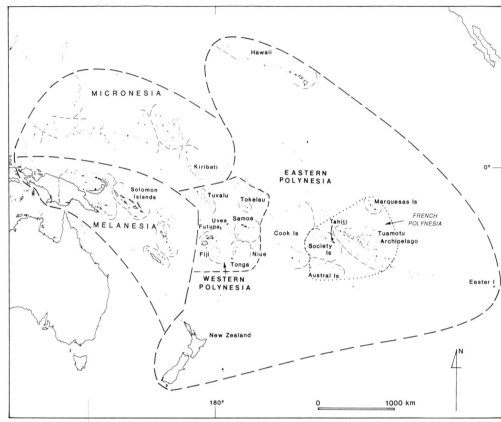

1. Map of Oceania, showing its major divisions of Melanesia, Micronesia and Polynesia.

forms of song and dance. In the eighteenth century a superior form of double-canoe was developed in Fiji and quickly copied in Tonga and Samoa, to the extent of retaining the Fijian name. A pair of *lali* slit drums (for signalling arrivals) formed part of the normal sea-going equipment on the Fijian vessel, and it seems likely that the presence of such drums in Tonga and Samoa dates back to this era. Tonga conducted wars of conquest throughout the region and at different times held temporary control of Samoa, Niue, Uvea, Futuna and even some of the Outliers. Among the cultural effects was the introduction in these islands of the Tongan nose-flute and possibly also one form of slit drum called *nafa* (figure 2).

By contrast, a purely cultural influence among the nations of

Western Polynesia was exerted by Samoa in the second half of the nineteenth century, with at least two types of dance being adopted in Tonga, Tokelau, Uvea and Kiribati (formerly the Gilbert Islands), although not without some structural changes. In Tonga, for example, the numbers of performers in the Samoan *māʻuluʻulu* grew from an average of thirty (in Samoa itself) to more than a thousand, and the Samoan mat-drum accompaniment was replaced by a battery of large skin drums whose local name was that of a Tongan slit drum on the verge of obsolescence. Despite its foreign origin, the dance as a whole is now firmly established in Tonga's ongoing musical tradition.

In some respects the islands of Eastern Polynesia mirror those of Western Polynesia. They are scattered over many thousands of square kilometres of ocean, and their cultures are more diverse; wide geographical separation and reliance on favourable winds and currents were effective impediments to frequent inter-group travel, and local cultures tended to develop independently. These islands were settled later than those to the west (the last being New Zealand some eight hundred years ago), and their colonisers brought with them the accumulated skills of their

2. The last existing specimen of a Tongan *nafa* slit drum being carried into the palace grounds to lead a dance performance in honour of the king's birthday, 1973. The drum no longer exists. (Copyright: Richard Moyle.)

forebears. The skills of wood-carving, for example, reach their peak in this region. And, whereas in Western Polynesia wooden musical instruments tended to have plain surfaces, many flutes and drums from the east were intricately carved in ways which made them prized possessions and works of art in their own right; the prestige of some outstanding specimens was such that they were given personal names. The characteristic uses of musical instruments, particularly drums, contrasted with the islands to the west, where they tended to be slit drums beaten singly or in pairs for signalling (figure 3). In Eastern Polynesia, however, particularly in islands near the equator, slit drums were typically beaten in small groups, often together with skin drums, to accompany group dancing. Skin drums featured prominently in the elaborate and extensive religious rituals of the region or signalled stages in the proceedings.

Introduced instruments tended to be melodic, for example the ukulele (based on the four-string Portuguese *braguinha*) and the guitar, and quickly and successfully competed with indigenous instruments such as the flute. Because of their history and development within Polynesia, it is clear that the ukulele, steel guitar and slack-key guitar are now 'traditional' instruments, and accordingly they are included in this present volume. The expanding London Missionary Society inadvertently was itself the means of spreading the small hand-held *pātē* slit drum from Eastern Polynesia into Western Polynesia. Beginning in 1830, the pioneer missionary John Williams used converted Cook Islanders as 'native teachers' in Samoa; these teachers introduced their own slit drum, the *pātē*, which was and still is used to announce the local pastor's daily school, as well as other activities.

The differences between European and Polynesian music structure and theory are, predictably, considerable. Each is animated by, and sustained from, its own conceptual basis. Whereas European music — vocal and instrumental taken together — can be discussed in an abstract sense by practitioners, Polynesian music as a rule cannot: vocal and instrumental forms are conceived of as separate entities. This approach is reflected in the absence of any generic term for 'music' in the broad European sense.

One reason why Polynesian vocal music, in particular, achieves cultural importance concerns the belief in the power of the uttered word. Through the uttered word, in speech, chant or song, contact with supernatural powers could be established and those powers activated for either positive (such as healing,

3. (Above) A pair of Fijian *lali* at Bau Tailevu, 1959. (Copyright: Fijian Ministry of Information.) (Below) A pair of Samoan *lali* slit drums. Lotofaga village, Western Samoa, 1966. Length of nearer instrument 1015 mm (3 feet 4 inches). (Copyright: Richard Moyle.)

crop growth) or negative (such as sorcery) use. Poetry, whether sung or recited, represented a refined category of the uttered word and was an appropriate medium for entertaining, sexually stimulating or placating the gods. But, by the same token, any performance error was construed as an insult and therefore likely to produce some form of divinely caused misfortune to one's self, family or village. For this same reason, New Zealand Maori chants (called *waiata*) require an unbroken flow of sound from start to finish; this is achieved by the singers staggering their breath breaks. This high social importance attached to correct musical performance reached its peak in Eastern Polynesia, where, in parts of French Polynesia (Tahiti, the Marquesas, Austral and Tuamotu archipelagos), specialists in song and chant formed part of the local priesthood. On behalf of the community, these specialists were responsible for preserving the texts and understanding of local chants, for teaching them to members of younger generations and for performing them on appropriate occasions. Religious rituals were often accompanied by temple drums, and these specialists were also responsible for these instruments. In return for their services, the musical priests received special distributions of food, material goods and even parcels of land. (By contrast, the jew's harp and mouthbow, the musical instruments whose sounds came closest to those of the human voice, and which indeed were intended to be the medium for transmitting intimate verbal messages, apparently had no association with the supernatural or strict rules governing performance.)

The sound of a few instruments, notably Samoan conch trumpets, was formerly believed to represent the voice of war-gods, and the trumpets themselves were considered sacred in their own right. Certain instruments were also distinguished from others of the same types by receiving personal names or by being associated with particular individuals. As is discussed below, Western Polynesian slit drums belonging to prominent persons occasionally had personal names, and some received honours normally associated with high-ranking humans. And in Samoa and New Zealand, certain conch trumpets were reserved for particular announcements pertaining to a prominent local family. For example, in one village in American Samoa only members of the paramount chief's family were allowed to make announcements using the conch; and one Maori conch was so highly prized that it was sounded only at the birth of the firstborn of the local line of chiefs.

Sung poetry, particularly when presented together with dance, was also an important medium for entertaining mere mortals. A performance of song and dance in one's honour was, and still is, the highest artistic form of respect payable to any individual. It was no coincidence that, wherever they travelled throughout the Pacific in the eighteenth and nineteenth centuries, European explorers were treated to large-scale displays of dancing. On some occasions the respect was intensified by a host chief himself participating, often by beating the drums.

In Western Polynesian choral music the melody is not located in the part highest in pitch (equivalent to the soprano) but in the second-lowest part. A parallel situation exists in performance by pairs of *lali* slit drums from this region, wherein the lower-pitched of the two drums performs the characteristic rhythmic pattern appropriate to the occasion while the higher-pitched instrument provides a steady rhythmic 'background'. Likewise, in groups of Tongan conch trumpets, the lead part is taken by the shell second lowest in pitch.

Vocal integration and instrumental integration tend to co-exist, so that, in island groups where ensembles of different types of musical instruments (or different-sized specimens of the same type of instrument) perform together, group songs containing more than one voice-part are also found. This occurs in, for example, Tonga, French Polynesia and the Cook Islands. The reverse also applies: island groups whose choral music is sung in unison tend to have either groups of the same musical instrument playing together (for example, Hawaii) or single instruments (for example, New Zealand).

Most types of instruments were associated with dance. Relatively few dances, however, were accompanied solely by instruments; it was more common for them to be performed together with group songs. From a purely practical point of view, it is not surprising that dance instruments tended to be of the percussion type, as a loud sound was necessary to penetrate the noise of body movements and singing and so provide a beat by which the dancers could synchronise their actions. Because such dances themselves incorporated the combined talents of poet, composer and choreographer, they represented possibly the most highly valued form of artistic expression. So great was the esteem in which such dances were held that, in some instances, the position of drummer was reserved for a high-ranking chief. Among island nations where social classes were clearly defined, certain forms of song and dance, as well as certain musical instruments, were reserved for individuals of chiefly rank, thus giving visual expression to, and thereby reinforcing, the social structure by means of creative artistry. The banning by nineteenth-century Protestant missionaries of several dance forms and the introduction of European instruments lacking any association with social prestige have combined to reduce the social importance of the drummer's identity.

Although individual women achieved high personal status, Polynesian leadership was, and still is, male-dominated. The performance of musical instruments, likewise, is largely a male domain, whether to accompany song and dance (for example, drums) or for personal amusement (for example, flutes).

The overall musical repertoire of an island nation does not usually comprise a scattered collection of completely unrelated styles, musical forces and values. On the contrary, it is generally unified by several elements recurring in the various categories of vocal and instrumental music. Instrumental and vocal music may be linked in one or more ways. Perhaps the most common link is for melodic instruments to join with singers in performing a melody. Early descriptions of group singing in Tahiti and Hawaii report flutes playing together with the singers. In but a single development of this situation, we also find flutes performing vocal melodies on their own, usually solo, but occasionally in groups. Clearly, in both situations, the tuning of the flutes must match the pitches of the songs. In Western Polynesia, from where the greatest number of bamboo nose-flutes have been collected, it is evident that the particular construction technique used tended to produce similar, if not identical, tunings. These tunings in turn matched the pitches of songs preserved since ancient times, thus giving continuity in both the vocal and instrumental repertoires. In contrast to the simple construction of bamboo instruments, solid wooden, bone or stone mouth-flutes from New Zealand took many hours of skilled labour to produce, and many more to finish with elaborate carving. Particular scales were in wide use and corresponded to the more common scales found in Maori chant; the maker's desire to achieve a particular tuning is sometimes evident in a flute in which a fingerhole has been plugged, apparently because it produced an incorrect pitch. Another obvious relationship between vocal and instrumental music is shared terminology. In Tonga individual shells in an ensemble of conch trumpets are given the same names that in vocal music correspond to soprano, alto, tenor and bass.

Change, which is part of Polynesian culture generally, has tended to affect indigenous musical instruments by substituting alternatives rather than by local development; that is, they existed in a relatively unchanged form before being either discontinued as a result of local social conditions or displaced by imported instruments. Within individual island groups instruments shared uniformly their means of construction and basic style while showing more individuality in non-functional elements, such as decoration. Although much of the story of Polynesian musical instruments must be told using the past tense, recent cultural renaissances in Hawaii and New Zealand have resulted in a return to the manufacture and performance of traditional instruments. A broader stimulus to the retention of indigenous instruments was the establishment in 1972 of the South Pacific Arts Festival, a pan-Pacific gathering of performers of song, dance and drama held every four years, which has been successfully staged in Fiji, New Zealand, Papua New Guinea, Tahiti and Australia. On the basis of excellence of performance, individual singers, actors and instrumentalists compete for national representation. Additionally, some countries have established national dance theatres, and others have instituted annual national song and dance competitions, at which instrumental skills are recognised and rewarded. Islands within French Polynesia annually celebrate Bastille Day with vocal and instrumental music, and other groups commemorate their own political independence with annual public festivals of music. Tonga's annual celebration of the king's birthday includes dancing accompanied by song and instruments. Individual semi-professional troupes frequently visit Europe and Asia, and representative groups from Tonga, the Cook Islands and New Zealand toured European countries for the first time in 1988 as part of a travelling international music festival. Within Polynesia itself, dance troupes frequently travel between Tahiti and the Cook Islands for tours lasting several weeks, and Samoan communities in New Zealand are often the hosts for visiting dance teams from Samoa seeking funds for village projects. Although there seems little chance that, without substantial changes to present cultural conditions, revived instruments can create for themselves an enduring and meaningful cultural niche among even more intense forms of the same outside influences which led to their earlier decline, all these occasions are grounds for cautious optimism about the continued existence and cultural importance of Polynesian musical instruments.

Technical terminology for instrument types and components has been avoided. When writing Polynesian words, two conventions have been followed: long vowels are marked with a macron (for example, *pātē*), and the glottal stop is indicated by an inverted comma (for example, *tō'ere*).

2
Percussion instruments

Slit drums

In their size, manner of beating and use, slit drums in Western Polynesia differ from those in Eastern Polynesia.

Most slit drums in Western Polynesia are made from single blocks of wood in an approximate boat shape, hollowed out with adze and fire to form a central resonating cavity. They are beaten with one or two small sticks, or with two sturdy shaped beaters, or struck end-on with a single large beater. A feature of Polynesian wooden slit drums generally is the presence at each end of a small cavity paralleling the depth and width of the central slit. Called 'ears' in some regions, these cavities are said to improve the drum's sound.

The pairs of slit drums called *lali* found in several island groups evidently originated from Fiji, where they were beaten to signal a wide variety of activities in times of peace and war. The drums range in length from approximately 90 to 150 cm (3 to 5 feet). Many predetermined rhythmic codes existed until the early twentieth century, enabling hearers to identify the intended message from the particular rhythm being beaten. The drums are of unequal size and produce notes of different pitch; the larger, deeper-toned drum leads the performance, the smaller, higher-pitched instrument usually beating an unchanging fast background rhythm throughout. In earlier times each code had a distinguishing rhythmic motif which was repeated throughout the performance. Renowned drummers would vary these motifs without, however, totally obscuring the code. Although most codes were beaten on a pair of *lali*, at least one call, designed to intimidate a besieged enemy village, used up to six drums. In some instances the drums were raised from the ground on logs so as to increase their resonance.

Forming part of normal equipment on Fijian ocean-going double-canoes (where they served to announce arrivals), the *lali* were adopted in Tonga and Samoa (possibly in the late eighteenth century), where, until recently, the practice of rhythmic codes was maintained (figure 3). Still in use (particularly in Tonga) to announce church and village activities, the *lali* now beat slow signals. Belying their simple construction, the *lali* require considerable stamina to play for an extended period, and drummers frequently complain of numbness in their hands

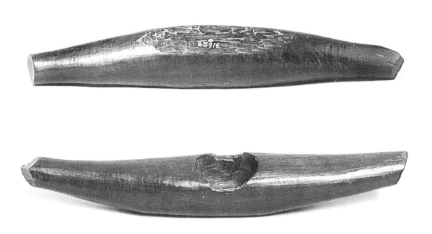

4. A Fijian *lali ni meke* slit drum. Length 450 mm (1 foot 5¾ inches). Note the bruising on the top where it was struck with two sticks. (Auckland Museum. Copyright: University of Auckland.)

as a result of the repeated jarring impact of wood against wood. Beating uses a combination of single hands in alternation and both hands simultaneously.

Both Tonga and Samoa possessed their own pre-*lali* slit drum called *nafa*, which was almost cylindrical in shape and had a very narrow slit. In size the *nafa* was similar to the *lali*. Beaten singly or in groups of two or three to accompany group songs and dances now obsolete, the *nafa* were reserved for men of high rank, and performance skill was valued. Talented Samoan drummers would demonstrate their dexterity to delight local audiences by clashing the drumsticks together or even tossing them into the air, while at the same time maintaining the beat. Struck with two beaters, the drum emitted different pitches at the ends and in the centre, so that tonal and rhythmic patterns could be established. In both regions, however, the drum was associated with dances now obsolete or virtually so, and the *nafa* has disappeared (figure 2). The last *nafa* in Tonga was beaten to accompany the sole surviving specimen of an ancient dance. Although performances were infrequent, the drum was left exposed to the elements and by 1980 had rotted and been replaced by a single *lali*. On Niue and Tuvalu, however, the *nafa* slit drum is still commonly used for signalling or accompanying dance, though without the association with high social status.

5. A large *logo* slit drum from Samoa together with its beater, collected by a Bishop Museum expedition in 1927. Length 3720 mm (12 feet 2½ inches). (Copyright: Bishop Museum, Honolulu.)

Fijian *lali* owned by paramount chiefs were themselves held in high esteem; in some areas they were given the name of a person and festivals were held in their honour. In other areas they had non-personal names (for example, Rumour of War). At least one Tongan *lali*, belonging to the country's first monarch, was named after a Fijian specimen. The naming of *lali* is also common in another medium, that of fiction. Throughout Western Polynesia there is a kind of spoken narrative told at night for domestic entertainment. It is common in such stories for *lali* to figure prominently in the plot, and most instruments are named, for example, 'Whistling in the Wind' or 'Tonga's Guardian'. (Until around the 1950s Tonga also had another kind of *lali*, which, despite its name, was not a slit drum but a solid length of wood placed over a hole dug in the ground and beaten with two sticks. It is said that most families had one of these drums and would play it for amusement in the cool of an evening.)

Fiji also has a much smaller slit drum used to accompany group song and dance. The *lali ni meke* ('dance *lali*') has a very small cavity excavated on one side (figure 4) but is turned over to play. It may be laid on the ground or held against an adult's chest to increase the resonance. Beaten by one of the singers, the *lali ni meke* has a distinctive bright sound.

Around the 1860s a very large single slit drum called *logo* (pronounced longo) appeared in Samoa, evidently based on the shape of the *lali* but intended as a substitute for a metal church bell; its sole use was — and still is — to announce religious services, and its low-pitched slow beats are audible for several kilometres (figure 5). The *logo*, easily the largest of Polynesia's slit drums, is struck with a single beater, similar in shape to an oversize baseball bat. Single, evenly spaced beats are struck against the side of the drum or on the lip; the sounds from large *logo* are extremely low-pitched and may be felt rather than heard. An indication of the size and weight of the instrument may be gained by noting that one particular *logo* made in 1928 for the Bishop Museum required seventy men to haul it rough-hewn to the sea, whence it was floated to the village; fourteen days were required to complete construction. As recently as the 1960s, most Samoan villages possessed at least one *logo*, sometimes housing them in special thatched shelters for protection from the rain. Today, however, few specimens remain, the others having been replaced by metal bells or empty oxygen

6. A *logo telie* slit drum from Niue, and its single beater. Hakupu village, 1984. Length 1680 mm (6 feet 6 inches). (Copyright: Richard Moyle.)

7. (Above) Two Samoan *pātē* slit drums. (Copyright: Richard Moyle.) (Below) Five bamboo *pātē* slit drums from Samoa. Patamea village, Western Samoa, 1968. (Copyright: Richard Moyle.)

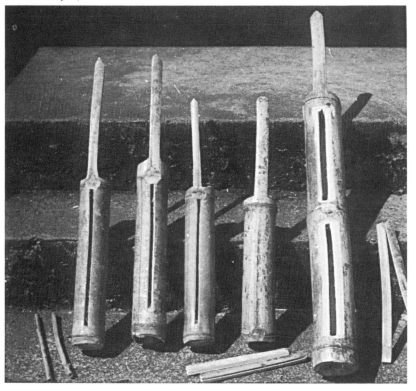

cylinders. Returning home after completing their theological training in Samoa, students from neighbouring Niue introduced to their own island a smaller version of the Samoan instrument, called *logo telie* after the *telie* tree from which it was made. On Niue also the drum is beaten principally to announce church services (figure 6).

Together with Christianity's arrival in Western Polynesia in the 1830s came a hand-held slit drum, the *pātē* (figure 7). This was introduced from Rarotonga in the Cook Islands, from where many converts to Christianity evangelised as 'native teachers' alongside British Protestant missionaries. As in the Cook Islands, so too wherever these teachers travelled within Western Polynesia (Samoa, Tokelau, Tuvalu), and also into Melanesia, the *pātē* was taken and beaten to announce the daily catechism schools which the teachers themselves administered. It was either held in one hand by the handle and struck with the other hand or held in two hands by another person, and the resonant sounds of the *pātē* still echo through villages in lasting tribute to the early teachers' evangelistic success. It is usually beaten in a fast unchanging rhythm by children at the command of an adult. Although most are carved from solid wood, bamboo specimens are also found (figure 7).

In sharp contrast to the essentially religious use of the *pātē* hand-held slit drum in Western Polynesia, use in Eastern Polynesia is predominantly to accompany secular drum dances (although the drum also functions to announce certain local church activities). All slit drums in this region are of this type. Beaten as part of a drum ensemble which includes one or more single-headed skin drums and one double-headed skin drum, and possibly also an empty kerosene can or tin for cabin-bread (a tough durable biscuit), groups of from three to eight (or even more) slit drums are organised according to the pitches of their instruments and play extremely fast sequences of tightly synchronised rhythmic patterns, forming solid blocks of sound (figure 8). The former small adzes are now replaced by chisels and even chainsaws as the drums are shaped from solid wood. The musical aesthetics of drum ensembles are such that, ideally, each slit drum should have its own separate pitch. Tuning is achieved during construction by varying the length of the slit, resulting in a battery of drums each of slightly different overall size. Each slit drum produces two distinct sounds: using a single stick, a loud resonant sound is generated when struck directly on the slit, and a softer tapping sound when struck on the drum's solid end. When the performers are seated, smaller drums are balanced on the inner surface of the forearm or stood on the thigh, while larger specimens are stood on end or laid flat on the ground. Professional groups, such as those performing regularly in hotels or nightclubs, tend to stand to play, their drums mounted horizontally in specially built frames. The ensemble is led by the smallest slit drum (often replaced nowadays by an empty tin), whose drummer alone may use two sticks, and whose very fast beat (eight hundred or more beats per minute) forms a reference point for the other performers. Drummers memorise their rhythmic sequences and the changes in striking location by a series of spoken nonsense syllables whose sounds and rhythms imitate those of the drumbeats themselves. Each drum dance is named (for example, 'The Duck', 'Manihiki Woman'), and the speech rhythm of the name forms the basis of the slit drums' opening rhythmic sequence.

Typical performance of a drum dance starts with a call from the leader, sometimes answered by the group. A single slit drum begins with a short rhythmic motif, repeating it as the other slit drums, either one after the other or as a unit, enter with the same motif. The point of entry of the skin drums varies from one dance to the next. When the group has repeated the motif a set number of times, with or without variations, they all abruptly stop and another motif is introduced from a single drum. The dancers' movements are synchronised to the drum rhythms and combine actions imitative of the composition's theme with 'basic' actions — women's rapid hip movements and men's fast scissor movements of the legs. The overall form of the music is sectional, and rhythmic complexity may be increased by the simultaneous playing of more than one rhythmic motif, building up to a frenzied climax. Both individual sections and the performance itself end abruptly. A larger Cook Islands slit drum existed until the earlier twentieth century. This drum differed from the smaller instruments in that its slit took the form of an elongated figure of eight, and it was beaten with two sticks; by beating at different points on its body a total of four pitches could be produced. Although this drum is now obsolete, it survives in the form of 'ghost voices', nocturnal sounds of singing and drumming which are said to be audible only to elderly islanders, and which are interpreted as a sign that a local chief is about to die.

A different kind of slit drum existed in New Zealand, although not all accounts agree about its construction. The Maori *pahū* was an oblong length of wood some 2 metres (6 feet 3 inches)

8. A small ensemble of Cook Islands drummers. Atiu island, 1988. (Copyright: Jenny Little.)

long suspended at each end by a length of flax cord attached to a frame mounted in the watch-tower of a fortified village. In the centre of the wood was a slot (or, in some descriptions, a deep groove) into which a wooden mallet was inserted and moved back and forth so as to strike the sides. Beating this drum signalled to the village's occupants that an enemy force was approaching, and accounts speak of its sound carrying as much as 30 km (19 miles) on a still day. Some specimens appear to have been struck with a heavy club on their outer surface. One reported variant form of *pahū* was made from a living hollow tree by cutting a tongue up to 9 metres (30 feet) long out of the standing trunk. Striking the tongue in different places reputedly produced a series of three or four different pitches.

Sounding board

'Sounding board' is the name given to two distinct types of instrument found in Western Polynesia. The instrument is identical in Tonga and Samoa: a long sliver is removed from a thin length of hardwood and then replaced, held in position by sennit (coconut fibre) cord threaded at each end through holes drilled

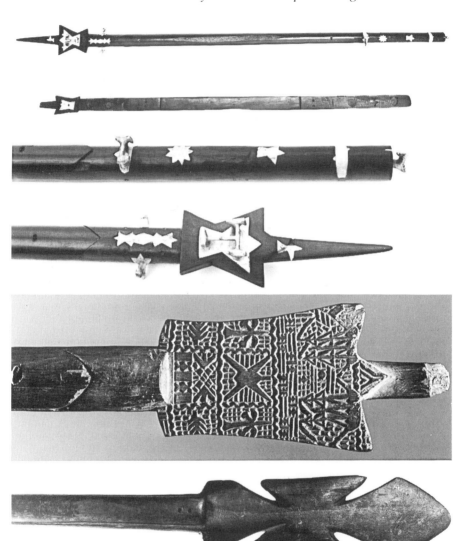

9. (Top) Two Tongan sounding boards (length of upper specimen 1332 mm, 4 feet 4 inches), with detail of each end of upper specimen, showing slat ends and whale-ivory inserts. (Auckland Museum. Copyright: University of Auckland.) (Centre) End section of a Tongan sounding board, showing slat end and attachment hole. (Copyright: National Museum of Ethnology, Leiden, Netherlands.) (Bottom) End section of a Samoan sounding board, showing slat end and attachment holes. (Copyright: Museum of Mankind, London.)

10. Detail from an illustration made in 1777 by John Webber entitled 'A Night Dance by Men in Hapaee [Ha'apai]'. Instruments played by the seated Tongan musicians include stamping tubes and what appears to be a sounding board.

in both the base and the slat. When laid slat uppermost on the ground and beaten with two light sticks, the slat rattles against the base, producing a high-pitched penetrating sound which, together with song, accompanied dances which were eventually banned by nineteenth-century missionaries. Only four Tongan and one Samoan specimen are known to exist (figure 9). The function of the whale-ivory protrusions on three Tongan specimens is unknown. The Tongan name for the instrument has passed out of use, but in Samoa it translated as 'chiefly thing', reflecting the high status of the performer. The man beating the board in Tonga also led the overall performance, and the position was reserved for an individual of high status. As with the indigenous Tongan slit drum, the *nafa*, performance was considered difficult to master, and skilled individuals were singled out for particular praise (figure 10).

The term 'sounding board' is also applied to a very different instrument on Bellona Island (in the Solomon Islands), in the Outliers, where it is a hardwood plank, crescent-shaped and convex (figure 11). Propped on the drummer's feet and resting against a stake in the ground, the board is struck with two stout beaters to produce a sound which, together with song, accom-

11. A sounding board on Bellona Island beaten to accompany a *kapa* dance. (Copyright: Jane Mink Rossen.)

panies particular categories of dance. Most of the beating occurs in the centre of the board, although higher tones are produced by striking close to the ends. Labelling indigenous dances as 'heathen', the dominant Protestant church on Bellona prohibits its members from participating, on pain of a fine or temporary excommunication. Because of the considerable cultural influence of the church, the future of both these dances and the sounding board itself is uncertain.

Stamping tube

The stamping tube is a section of stout bamboo with all but one node removed. When held perpendicularly with the closed end down and struck down on to the ground or a pad, the tube emits a low dull sound which marks the pulse of the song which it accompanies (figure 12). Although once common in several parts of Polynesia, the stamping tube is now found only in Fiji and Hawaii, used in association with dance songs. If tuning is desired (as was apparently the case in nineteenth-century Tonga when several tubes sounded together), this is easily accomplished by trimming the overall length. The tubes are usually sounded simultaneously.

From illustrations of Tongan tubes seen in use by Captain Cook's men in the 1770s (figure 10), it is evident that they could

12. Together with singing and beating a *lali ni meke* (see figure 4), Fijian stamping tubes accompany a dance. Waitabu village, Lau, 1977. (Copyright: Richard Moyle.)

13. Four Tokelauan men strike a box drum and another beats an empty tin to accompany a *fātele* dance. (Copyright: Ken George.)

reach a height of almost 2 metres (6 feet) and were played in groups of two to five. One description from Tonga notes that tubes of different lengths were thumped at the same time to produce a kind of muffled chord. Hawaiian specimens tend to be around 50 cm (1 foot 8 inches) tall and are hit on the ground or a mat by kneeling dancers, who hold a tube in each hand. In recent years the tubes have occasionally featured among the accompanying instruments for Hawaiian popular songs.

Box drum

A development in the three atolls comprising Tokelau is the box drum (*pōkihi*, from the English 'box'). Presumably originating as a discarded wooden box laid on the ground and struck with the hands, the instrument is now purpose-built. Made wide to allow several men to beat it together, and low to allow them to beat while seated, the plywood drum is covered with a mat or

tarpaulin which may be decorated (figure 13). For added resonance, empty tins, sometimes containing stones, may be placed
inside. The drum is used for the national *fātele* dance and is
placed behind the rows of standing dancers, among the separate
group of singers who boost the dancers' own singing. A large
empty tin is usually placed next to the box drum and beaten with
light sticks to emphasise the rhythm further. The two instruments
lead the overall acceleration of tempo characteristic of this
dance type. Belying its simple appearance, the drum must be hit
strongly in order to make it sound, and there have been instances
when the drum has split under the combined impact of several
enthusiastic beaters. The drum has been recently introduced to
the neighbouring archipelago of Tuvalu for use in the *fātele*
dancing there.

Jew's harp

The name jew's harp is a misnomer: the instrument is not a
harp and has no known Jewish origin. It is, however, widely
reported within Polynesia. The instrument is typically made from
two parts of the coconut leaf, which naturally divides lengthwise
into two, separated by a midrib. One end of a section of leaf 10-

14. A Samoan boy playing a '*utete* or jew's harp. Patamea village, Western Samoa,
1969. (Copyright: Richard Moyle.)

15 cm (4 to 6 inches) long is gripped on edge between the teeth. A slightly longer length of midrib is held against this leaf, and the protruding end is twanged with the other hand (figure 14). The name within Western Polynesia, *'utete* (or a local variation), describes the performance technique: *'u* = grip with the teeth, and *tete* = vibrate. (By contrast, the same word in parts of Eastern Polynesia refers to the mouth-bow, now obsolete; both instruments use the principle of the mouth cavity serving to amplify the sound.)

Although played for personal amusement, the jew's harp is also said to have been used for private communication during courting: by forming particular vowel combinations with the mouth while playing, specific verbal messages could be transmitted. In most parts of Polynesia now, however, the instrument has either passed out of use or become a child's plaything.

Pebbles

Although clicking stones together may occasionally form the accompaniment for Samoan songs, the practice is more common in Hawaii. As an accompaniment for certain *hula* dances, each dancer holds two stones between the fingers of each hand and clicks them together in the manner of a pair of castanets.

Resonant sticks

Resonant sticks which come closer to being musical instruments in their own right are the Hawaiian *kāla'au*. As an accompaniment to certain *hula* dances, each dancer holds two hardwood sticks, striking the shorter (18-25 cm, 7-10 inches long) against the longer (90 cm, 3 feet) in set rhythms. Dancers also strike each other's sticks. In newer *hula* the sticks tend to be of equal length (25-30 cm, 10-12 inches).

Gourd rattle

Rattles are not common in Polynesia and are largely confined to Hawaii, where they are used to accompany *hula* dances. The *'ulī'ulī* consists of a coconut shell or gourd to which is attached a handle ending in a disc of barkcloth fringed with feathers. Pebbles, seeds or shells are placed inside the shell or gourd. The hand-held instrument is rotated rapidly to produce a constant sound, or struck against the body or palm of the other hand. In the eighteenth century rattles made of as many as a thousand dog teeth attached to a fibre mesh were worn below the knees by male *hula* dancers, whose movements caused the rattle to

15. A model using a gourd drum. (Drum: Honolulu Art Academy Association. Copyright: Bishop Museum, Honolulu.)

sound. More recently, shells have been substituted for dog teeth.

Gourd drum

Although the geographical area where gourds grow is broad, only in Hawaii are the resonating qualities of the empty shells used for musical purposes. The gourd drum consists of two gourds called *ipu*, one larger than the other. An opening 12-20 cm (5 to 8 inches) in diameter is cut into the top of the larger gourd, and a similar opening cut into both the bottom and the top of the smaller gourd. The two gourds are then joined, using local glue or by binding, to form a single instrument 50-90 cm (1 foot 8 inches to 3 feet) high. Some specimens have a cord looped around the join for carrying purposes.

The completed drum is also called *ipu*, and produces two distinct sounds. The player sits or kneels on the ground, behind a mat or cloth pad (figure 15). The drum is quickly lifted and thumped on to the pad, producing a deep tone. In the intervals between these beats the lower gourd is struck with the fingers of the other hand, producing a high sound, experienced players sometimes adding rhythmic ornaments produced by rapid slaps using fingers and thumb.

Percussion wand

An instrument unique to Hawaii is the split bamboo wand called *pū'ili*. A length of bamboo with one node removed is split down almost all of its length in fine (2-4 mm or ⅛-¼ inch) sections; the intact end with the node serves as a handle (figure 16). Like most of Hawaii's instruments, the *pū'ili* traditionally accompanies a *hula* dance. Chanting as they do so, the dancers move in unison, tapping the instrument against their own arm, or on the ground, or against a partner's shoulder or arm to produce a rustling sound. Modern specimens of this dance often feature standing performers with a *pū'ili* in each hand, sometimes striking them against each other.

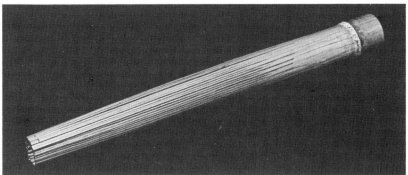

16. A Hawaiian *pū'ili* percussion wand. Length 515 mm (1 foot 8 inches). (Auckland Museum. Copyright: University of Auckland.)

Foot-activated instruments

Although rhythmic stamping occurs in vigorous men's dancing from several parts of Polynesia, foot-activated instruments are rare. The only indigenous instruments reported from Polynesia's easternmost island, Easter Island (or Rapanui), are the conch trumpet and the foot drum. The drum, now obsolete, was made by digging a hole about 1 metre (3 feet 3 inches) deep and 0.5 metre (1 foot 8 inches) wide. A large gourd, half-filled with cloth or grass, was placed in the hole, which was covered with a thin stone slab. A man stood on this slab, beating time with his

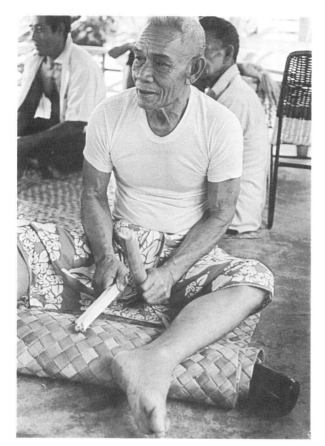

17. A Samoan mat drum, with empty bottles adding resonance. Solosolo village, Western Samoa, 1975. (Copyright: Ad and Lucia Linkels.)

feet as an accompaniment to dance.

The obsolete Hawaiian *papa hehi* treadleboard consisted of a wooden slab laid on a wooden crosspiece and used as a treadle, giving a hollow sound. The person playing the instrument also struck together a pair of hardwood sticks, the two complementary sounds acting as a timekeeper for *hula* dances on two of Hawaii's islands.

Mat drum

The mat drum (*fala*) accompanies several forms of secular choral singing throughout Western Polynesia. Formed by rolling a floor mat (approximately 80 by 200 cm or 2 feet 8 inches by 6 feet 6 inches) into a tube and holding it in place by tying or by placing one leg on it, the drum is beaten with two light sticks (figure 17). The sound may be amplified by inserting empty bottles (formerly lengths of bamboo) into the tube. After performance the mat reverts to its former use.

Body percussion

Polynesia's oldest musical instrument is also humanity's oldest — the human body. Body percussion takes three forms in Polynesia: clapping, slapping and flicking. Clapping together with song as an accompaniment to dance is characteristic of Western Polynesian music (although it is reported also from the Marquesas Islands in Eastern Polynesia). Two forms are used: with the hands held parallel and flat, and with the hands at right angles and cupped. The first gives a loud bright sound, whereas the other produces a dull thump. In some instances the choir practises and memorises the points in the song where the clapping changes from one form to the other. On other occasions the choir leader, who normally stands in the middle of the seated singers, signals both the changes and the speed of the clapping by using exaggerated gestures. In all cases the singers clap in unison using the same form. Simultaneous performance of the two different forms occurs in one category of Tongan song, in which the singers divide into three sections: one claps in a slow pulse using cupped hands, another has a slightly faster rhythm using flat hands, and the third part is even faster, again using flat hands. Two further forms of clapping as an accompaniment to song are reported from the Marquesas Islands: the fingers of one hand striking the palm of the other; and the left arm held crooked against the body and the cupped right hand struck against the hollow between the elbow and chest.

Body slapping takes three forms: seated singers may accompany themselves by slapping their thighs; standing dancers may incorporate synchronised thigh-slapping into their movements; and elaborate slapping may be formalised into a dance, the Samoan *fa'ataupati*. In this wordless standing dance the male performers execute a series of fast synchronised slaps to their sides (using the inner surface of their arms), chests (using open palms) and other parts of the body (figure 18). Performance rarely lasts more than a minute, and the physical exertion leaves the men with reddened chests and perspiring bodies. Thigh-slapping while seated is widely found in Polynesia. Periodic slapping of the thighs is choreographed in Maori *haka* posture dances. Such slapping occurs in the best known specimen of this dance, the one performed on the playing field by New Zealand's national rugby team, the All Blacks, before its games.

18. Samoan *fa'ataupati* dance. Apia, Western Samoa, July 1979. (Copyright: Ad and Lucia Linkels.)

Flicking has been reported from the northern Cook Islands, as a form of children's amusement. The mouth forms the shape for the sound 'o' as in 'often', and the fingers of both hands flick along the upper lip, both cheeks and the lower lip, which produces a variety of sounds which resonate inside the mouth cavity. The flickering is in time to the words of a short text.

The mouth cavity acts as a resonator for a further type of instrument (see also the jew's harp, above). In New Zealand and the northern Cook Islands one end of a piece of narrow wood is held in the mouth and the other end tapped with a second stick. The resultant sounds are modified by changing the shape of the mouth cavity as the stick is tapped. In New Zealand the instrument was formerly used to accompany special songs, whereas in the northern Cooks it is a child's plaything.

Skin drum

The skin drum is principally an instrument of Eastern Polynesia. Whether beaten by hand or sticks, whether single or

19. Detail from an illustration made in 1777 by John Webber entitled 'A Dance at Otaheite [Tahiti]'. The three drummers are playing a combination of high-footed and low-footed drums.

double-headed, the drum in former times functioned as a signalling device or as an accompaniment to song and dance (figure 19). Present-day use is confined to the latter. Until cattle and goats were introduced in the earlier twentieth century, the drum head was made of sharkskin and in the Cook Islands this material is reflected in the drum's name, *pau mango* ('sharkskin drum'). Whatever the type of skin, however, the head was secured to the body by sennit cord. A series of holes was made around the circumference of the skin and sennit was threaded through these, passing down to holes near the base of the drum, where it looped around and returned up for threading through the next hole. In some specimens one length of sennit was threaded loosely through all the holes around the circumference, forming a series of small loops; other lengths were then threaded through these loops and attached to the base.

Many older specimens are known technically as footed drums, because the resonating chamber rests on a circular foot, the whole instrument being carved from a single piece of wood. The concave, solid wooden septum forming the base of the resonating chamber can be seen clearly in figure 20. Carved into the resonating chamber of some old specimens from the Cook Islands is a protrusion in the shape of a tongue, which is said to give the drum its appropriate sound.

Specimens collected near the time of European contact were of two basic shapes: short and rather squat, and tall and narrow.

These narrow specimens are arguably the tallest skin drums in the whole of Oceania, some being more than 2 metres (6 feet) in height and requiring the drummer to stand on a platform. In addition to accompanying artistic performances, the drums also signalled stages of religious rituals. On Tahiti the largest drum of all, the *tō'ere*, was beaten to announce rituals of human sacrifice, and early European visitors wrote with dread of the distinctive sound of this instrument. (With the eventual abolition of the rituals, the drums became obsolete, but the name *tō'ere* was transferred to the small slit drum now used to accompany drum dances.)

According to legend, the Hawaiian *pahu* was brought from

20. (Left) A Tahitian drum. Height 405 mm (1 foot 4 inches). (Copyright: National Museum of Ireland, Dublin.) (Right) An eighteenth-century Hawaiian *pahu* skin drum. The sharkskin drum head is held by tension cords of braided five-ply coconut fibre. On the drum's foot an upper row of nine dancing figures (showing nine extra heads to double the impression of numbers) is supported by a second row of nine whose heads are turned to one side to indicate the strain. Height 470 mm (1 foot 6½ inches). (Copyright: Canterbury Museum, Christchurch, New Zealand.)

Tahiti some six hundred years ago by Laka, the patron deity of the *hula* dance. Initially used for temple worship, where it accompanied chanting and was kept in a special house, the drum later also accompanied the *hula pahu* dances appropriate for this type of music. The rhythms, which ranged from improvisatory to a simple pulse, were also of varying timbre, produced by beating with two hands on different parts of the drum head. Because of the religious associations of the *pahu*, the *hula pahu* is regarded as the highest form of dance expression.

The smallest Polynesian skin drum is probably the Hawaiian *pūniu*, a coconut shell covered with a skin and attached to the lower thigh by means of a short rope. The drummer struck this with braided fibre while beating the larger *hula pahu* skin drum with the other hand (figure 21). Unlike other Hawaiian accom-

21. A model using a *hula* drum (*pahu hula*) and a small knee drum (*pūniu*). (Copyright: Bishop Museum, Honolulu.)

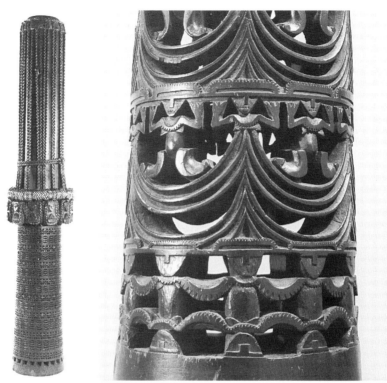

22. (Left) An Austral Islands *pahu rā* drum. Height 1300 mm (4 feet 3 inches). (Auckland Museum. Copyright: University of Auckland.) (Right) Detail from the foot of an Austral Islands drum. (Metropolitan Museum of Art, New York. Copyright: Charles Uht.)

panying instruments, the *pūniu* is not used on its own. The drum is still manufactured and used as part of Hawaii's cultural renaissance.

Although modern specimens tend to be plain, drums collected in the eighteenth and nineteenth centuries contain some of the most detailed carving of any type of Polynesian instrument. The most intricate carving comes from the Austral Islands (figure 22).

The development of the drum dance in French Polynesia and the Cook Islands featuring movement in time to an ensemble of slit and skin drums has produced rather different types of skin drum. A large two-headed drum, seated in a wooden frame or suspended from a tree or gable and struck with a single padded beater, provides the pulse for the ensemble. Individual drums are often given personal names (for example 'Lady Baden-Powell') and referred to by these names rather than by the local equivalent of the word *pahu*. These drums are usually made from the hollowed base of a coconut palm trunk and, because the trunk widens at its base, the diameter of one head tends to be greater than that of the other. Typical ensembles also contain one or more free-standing single-headed drums, similar in shape to a tall bongo drum and struck with two light sticks to provide a counter-rhythm to the principal rhythm of the set of slit drums.

Tonga alone in Western Polynesia has its own stick-beaten skin drums, called *nafa*. Made from a halved barrel or metal drum, one or more of the drums accompanies the *mā'ulu'ulu* dance. If there are several drums, the largest (possibly together with one or more smaller ones) is beaten by the drum leader. The opening section of this dance features the drums alone; against a constant background from the smaller instruments, the leader here beats a series of virtuosic rhythms, coloured streamers attached to his drumsticks adding a visual element to the sonic display. When the dancing and singing begin, however, the drums retreat to a time-keeping role.

On the small island of Uvea a local dance form called *eke* developed, featuring quartets of stick-wielding men who sang as they clashed their sticks against those of their companions, in imitation of the movements of hand to hand fighting. The dance spread to Tonga in the 1830s and later to the Lau archipelago of Fiji, as well as to Samoa and Tokelau. Although performance in these other areas is not frequent, and the movements and accompanying songs have undergone change, the rhythm of the clashing sticks continues to help unite the dancers' movements; despite being dance implements, the sticks additionally function as musical instruments in this context.

3
Wind instruments

Conch trumpet

The use of the conch trumpet in Oceania is as wide as the natural distribution of the *Bursa bubo*, *Charonia tritonis* and *Cassis cornuta* shells, from which the instrument is made. Because of the coldness of its coastal waters, these shells were not found in New Zealand; conches there were initially of the smaller *Charonia lampas capax* shell until European ships brought the larger *tritonis* specimens as trade items in the eighteenth and nineteenth centuries.

Initial construction is virtually identical throughout the region. For the *Charonia tritonis* and *Charonia lampas capax* a single hole is drilled or knocked in the fourth or fifth whorl from the point (those nearer the end being solid). New Zealand Maori specimens intended to carry a mouthpiece had the entire tip of the shell removed. For the *Cassis cornuta*, the stubby knob on the circular end of the shell is knocked off. Within Western Polynesia, the hole is then placed against the lips and blown using the same technique as for a European brass instrument. Within many of the island groups of Eastern Polynesia, however, a mouthpiece was added. In New Zealand this mouthpiece was made from solid wood and often heavily carved (figure 23); attached by means of a mastic, it continued the direction of the point of the shell. Bamboo was used in tropical islands, in which case the blowing hole was pierced in the side of the shell tip and the mouthpiece mounted perpendicularly from this hole, sometimes secured with guy cords. Because of the fragility of the bamboo and its means of attachment, few museum specimens with bamboo mouthpiece intact appear to have survived (figure 23).

Bursa bubo specimens from one part of Fiji are unique in that they have thick fibre handles and one fingerhole (figure 24). Fingering this hole while blowing changes the pitch by the interval of approximately a whole tone (or major second).

The most common use of the conch is as a signalling device, its loudness and portability lending versatility. On land it announced, and in many regions continues to announce, a very wide variety of secular and religious events within the village, from the nightly curfew to the availability of freshly baked bread. One remarkable use occurs on the death of a high chief

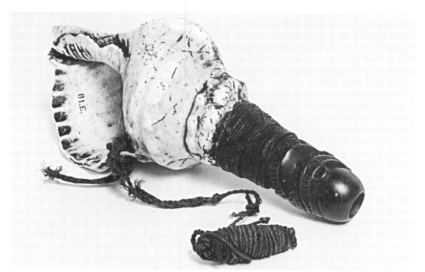

23. (Above) A Maori *pūtātara* conch trumpet (*Charonia lampas capax*), with wooden mouthpiece and plaited fibre plug. (Auckland Museum. Copyright: University of Auckland.) (Below) A conch trumpet (*Charonia tritonis*) from the Marquesas Islands. The mastic around the blowing hole formerly held in place a wooden or bamboo mouthpiece. (Copyright: Musée de l'Homme, Paris.)

24. A Fijian *Bursa bubo* conch trumpet from the island of Viti Levu. Length of shell 210 mm (8 inches). (Auckland Museum. Copyright: University of Auckland.)

in Fiji, when shells are blown continuously by relays of people in an unbroken signal from the time of death until the burial. In one documented case, because of a delay in the arrival of an eminent mourner, the body lay unburied for an entire month, during which time the conches sounded unceasingly. Grieving noblemen in parts of Fiji were not permitted to wail but instead blew a conch, whose own sound was considered to be that of wailing. On the sea, the instrument is principally used in communal spear-fishing drives; the leader remains in his canoe and uses the trumpet to ensure that the divers work as a group. Whatever the context of the signal, the conch sounds the fundamental pitch only; although harmonics are possible they are not blown.

In Tonga the conch has the additional function of a genuine musical instrument. Although once common throughout the kingdom, such use is largely confined to one northerly island. Groups of three to seven (or even more) male conch players gather, each with his own shell (figure 25). The leader listens to the pitch of each shell and, if two or more are similar, he will direct the higher instrument(s) to tune to the lower by placing a hand in the mouth of the shell, just as a French-horn player stops his instrument by thrusting a hand into the bell. When the pitches are organised, each part is assigned a short rhythm which is then repeated for the duration of the performance. Perform-

25. A group of Tongans with *Charonia tritonis* conch trumpets. Falehau village, Tonga. (Copyright: University of Auckland.)

ance is structured so that, as one player takes a breath, at least one other continues to blow, producing a constant flow of sound that can continue for hours at a time. The only known use for the conch ensembles is as a means of sustaining excitement at inter-village cricket matches (the game was introduced in the nineteenth century); no pre-cricket use appears to have been recorded.

Panpipes

Panpipes are confined to parts of Western Polynesia, where they have been obsolete since around the beginning of the twentieth century. It may or may not be coincidental that these same islands are the closest to Melanesia, where the instrument is in widespread and common use. Although several specimens were collected by early European visitors, especially from Tonga (figure 26), little information on performance practice exists; it appears that Tongans were reluctant to use the pipes in the presence of Europeans. Indeed, William Ellis, one of Captain Cook's crew in the 1770s, noted: 'Though this instrument was very common among them, we seldom saw them use it.' The pipes, which are all closed by a node at their non-blowing end, lie in a single raft lashed together with sennit cord.

Tongan panpipes in particular are distinguished by the unevenness of their pipes (that is, they do not lie from shortest to longest), and those from Tonga and Samoa by the bevel on the blowing end of each tube, whereas those from Melanesia have flat ends. The bevel has the effect of focusing the airflow on to single pipes. Because of the nature of their acoustics, the pitches of panpipes, even those with pipes now unplayable, can be determined from their physical measurements. From similarities in the tunings of panpipes from Tonga, the only region where detailed research has been undertaken, it appears that the pitches represent the outline of a stereotyped melody existing also in solo songs. According to this theory, the player begins at one end of the panpipes and proceeds towards the other, with occasional direction reversals as required by the melody.

26. Tongan panpipes. (Copyright: National Museums of Scotland, Edinburgh.)

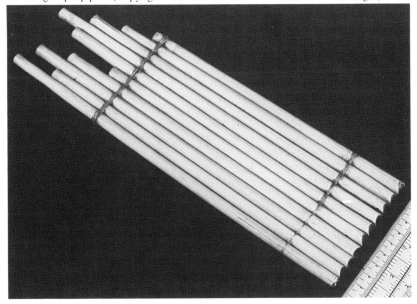

By contrast, the pipes in specimens from Fiji and Samoa (figure 27) are placed in order from shortest to longest and, in common with the Melanesian pattern, Fijian pipes are held rigid by a crosspiece lashed in place on either side of the raft.

Nose-flute

Although the nose-flute was once used throughout Polynesia (with the apparent exception of New Zealand and Easter Island) as a means of private entertainment, two distinct forms emerged, corresponding to the two major cultural divisions of the region. With the exception of some specimens from Niue, flutes are made of bamboo, and indeed the most common term for the instrument in Polynesia is the same word as for bamboo, for example *kofe, kohe, 'ofe, ohe.*

Western Polynesian nose-flutes appear to be based on the

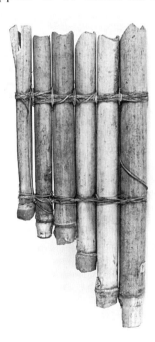

27. Samoan panpipes. Length of longest pipe 170 mm (6½ inches). (Copyright: Museum für Völkerkunde, Dresden.)

28. Fijian nose-flute. Length 660 mm (2 feet 2 inches). (Auckland Museum. Copyright: University of Auckland.)

29. The late Veʻehala of Tonga, playing his *fangufangu* nose-flute. (Copyright: *Sydney Morning Herald.*)

Fijian instrument, which is a length of stout bamboo closed at each end by a node, and containing five equidistant holes stretching along a single plane (figure 28). Spaced equidistantly around the circumference, at the point where the central of these five holes is positioned, are a further three holes (in cross-section: at the 3, 6 and 9 o'clock positions). Only the holes nearest and furthest from the blowing hole are fingered, giving a tonal inventory of four pitches. The flute may be blown from either end, although some players prefer the end where the node is convex, which allows a closer fit. To play, the flute is held against the upper lip so that the blowing hole lies just below one nostril (figure 29). The thumb of one hand closes the other nostril, while the second or third finger of that hand operates the closest fingerhole. The other hand holds the non-blowing end and operates another fingerhole.

In the late eighteenth century the five equidistant holes of Tongan flutes were not in a single plane (figure 30) but had the second and fourth some 10 degrees to the left or right; a sixth hole lay on the underside, directly opposite the third. Whatever the reason for this placement, it was apparently replaced in the nineteenth century by five equidistant holes in a single plane,

30. An eighteenth-century Tongan *fangufangu* nose-flute. Length 568 mm (1 foot 10½ inches). (Copyright: National Museums of Scotland, Edinburgh.)

together with the sixth on the underside; this arrangement has continued to the present day. (The five holes are positioned by measuring with string the distance between the nodes. Folding the string in half gives the position for the central hole, and halving it again locates the remaining two holes.) Counting the blowing hole as number one, it is normal practice to finger holes two and five. The flute was formerly used to accompany song and for personal amusement. It was also used to awaken slumbering royalty. (The last occasion this was done was in 1953, when Queen Elizabeth II and the Duke of Edinburgh stayed overnight in the Tongan palace and were woken at dawn by four flute players on the verandah.)

The nose-flute is now obsolete in neighbouring Samoa, Tokelau, Uvea and Futuna. Evidence from Samoa indicates that, unlike Tonga, there was variety in the number and location of fingerholes (figure 31). The local name for the flute in most of Western Polynesia was *fangufangu*, which derives from *fangu*,

31. A Samoan nose-flute. Length 371 mm (1 foot 2½ inches). (Copyright: Royal Albert Memorial Museum, Exeter.)

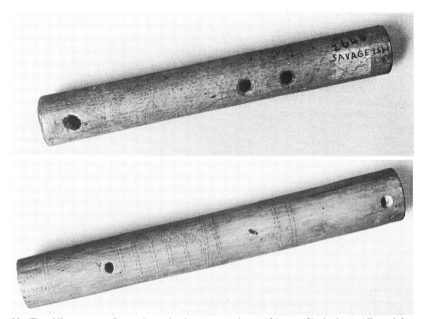

32. Two Niuean nose-flutes. Length of upper specimen 138 mm (5½ inches). (Copyright: Victoria Museum, Melbourne.)

'to blow'. The island of Niue, however, is an exception.

Although the nineteenth-century name for the Niuean flute was the word for bamboo (*kofe*), the terms for the flute and for bamboo have now changed to two entirely different words. The nose-flute on Niue is called *kilikihoa* (or *kikihoa*), an apparently designative term. Unlike flutes from other locations in Polynesia, the Niuean flute may be of bamboo or wood. Wooden specimens are made from a tree branch whose pith is removed after drying. Both bamboo and wooden flutes are open at the non-blowing end and have two fingerholes in a single plane approximately 50 per cent and 60 per cent respectively along the length of the instrument (figure 32). Both fingerholes are fingered using the same hand (figure 33). Only one flute player is still alive and, through lack of local interest, the instrument appears about to become obsolete. Although Niue lies within Western Polynesia, the open-ended construction and the placement of the fingerholes on its flutes make Niuean instruments similar to flutes from Eastern Polynesia.

Throughout the Cook Islands and the archipelagos of French Polynesia the bamboo nose-flute, now obsolete, was called *vivo*.

33. Talaiti, the last player of the Niuean nose-flute. Vaiea village, 1984. (Copyright: Richard Moyle.)

The flutes had two to four fingerholes, usually clustered some two-thirds of the way along the instrument's length, and were distinguished principally by differences in the size of the holes (figure 34). Some holes are as small as 2 mm (⅛ inch) in diameter and may be positioned very close to larger holes, suggesting that the small holes may have been fingered together with the larger ones, or that they were used to produce micro-tones (melodic intervals smaller than a semitone). Support for this second possibility comes from early visitors' descriptions of flutes playing in unison with songs whose own melodies contained very small shifts of pitch. When two Tahitian flutes playing together required tuning adjustments to achieve unison, a leaf was wrapped around the end of the shorter instrument to lengthen it and so lower its overall pitch to that of the other. In addition to personal amusement and accompanying certain forms of song, the flutes were played together with skin drums to accompany dancing. As with the jew's harp elsewhere in Poly-nesia, the nose-flute in the Marquesas Islands is said to have been able to communicate precise verbal messages during court-ing.

Although modern specimens tend to have plain surfaces,

34. Two Tahitian nose-flutes, one with eight bindings of braided cord. Length of lower instrument 422 mm (1 foot 4½ inches). (Copyright: Cambridge University Museum of Archaeology and Anthropology.)

many flutes collected in the nineteenth century are heavily decorated with a wide variety of scratched or burnt lines, hatching, stars or even free-hand illustrations (figure 35). A few flutes from Tonga have the manufacturer's name and village burnt on with fine heated wire, together with one or more epigrams. Several flutes collected from Tahiti are distinguished by bands of sennit cord at points along their length (figure 34); these may have been for decoration or to impede cracking, a problem for all bamboo instruments when dry.

The pre-European association of the nose-flute with personal entertainment rendered it vulnerable to European musical instruments, particularly the guitar and ukelele, which had the same function. Indeed, the rise in popularity of the one was matched by a decline of the other. The additional uses of the flute — courting, awakening royalty, accompanying song and dance — were co-casualties of missionary and other forms of European influence. Although the nose-flute still exists in Tonga, Niue and Hawaii, these forms of competition do not augur well for its continued existence.

35. A Tongan *fangufangu* nose-flute with decorations burnt on with fine wire. Length 511 mm (1 foot 8 inches). (Copyright: Museum of Mankind, London.)

Mouth-flute

Polynesia has only two documented types of indigenous end-blown flute, and both are confined to New Zealand. (A mouth-blown flute, possibly end-blown, has been reported from several of the Cook Islands, but no specimens appear to have been collected.) Although technically known as end-blown, they are not held straight in front of the player (like, for example, a

recorder), but obliquely, some 20 degrees to one side and angled down. Several specimens are heavily carved and regarded as works of art in their own right; a few celebrated flutes were even given personal names. It was common practice to wear these types of flute on a cord around the neck as an ornament when not in use, and a shallow hole or lug was commonly found on the underside to allow insertion of the carrying cord.

The *kōauau* is a short tube rounded at the blowing end and with three unevenly spaced fingerholes. Most specimens are of hollowed wood, but some are of human or albatross bone (figure 36). It was believed that a supreme insult was paid to a defeated enemy, an ultimate defilement of his personal cosmological power, by fashioning a flute from one of his bones (usually the humerus). Specimens made from the humerus of an albatross come exclusively from the South Island, where, curiously, no Maori name for the instrument appears to have been recorded. A recent revival of interest in the instruments has rescued them from the point of obsolescence and resulted in many new specimens being made, most of wood but some using deer antler.

Perhaps the most famous of all *kōauau* was the one belonging to the young chief Tutanekai, who lived on the shore of Lake Rotorua. The sound of this flute so captivated the heart of the young woman Hinemoa when she heard it from Mokoia island, in the centre of the lake, that she swam to him. The *kōauau* is also mentioned in what is reputedly the world's longest place-name, Te Taumatawhakatangitangihangakōauautamateapokai-whenuakitanatahu, which translates as 'The brow of the hill where Tamatea-pokai-whenua played on his flute to his lady-love'.

Because neither cross-fingering (different combinations of open and closed holes) or partial holing (only partially closing a hole with the finger, creating a different pitch) was practised, the three fingerholes yielded a total of four pitches. Although at least nine four-note scales are known to have been used throughout New Zealand, two of these are found in almost two-thirds of all known extant specimens and produce a combination of semitones and whole tones. By comparing the flute scales with

36. (Opposite above) The front and rear of a heavily carved Maori *kōauau* flute. Length 145 mm (5¾ inches). (Auckland Museum. Copyright: University of Auckland.) (Below) A selection of *kōauau* made from (from the left) two species of wood, stone and albatross bone. (Auckland Museum. Copyright: University of Auckland.)

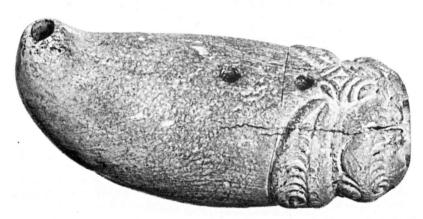

37. A Maori *nguru* mouth-flute made of whale ivory. Length 90 mm (3 inches). (Auckland Museum. Copyright: University of Auckland.)

the locations where they were collected and (with the aid of archaeology) the likely dates of manufacture, it is possible to determine that, between the eighteenth and twentieth centuries, five regional tuning systems existed. These systems in turn break down into three broad groups corresponding to the standard scales of many *waiata* chants, which is not surprising when one considers that the *kōauau* was used to play *waiata* melodies and also to accompany the unison singing of such chants.

The *nguru* flute has a large hole at the blowing end and a smaller hole at the other end, in the centre of a narrow upturned snout (figure 37). The instrument's unusual shape is suggestive of a whale tooth or small gourd, and the archaeological discovery of a gourd *nguru* adds weight to this possible theory of origin. Two additional fingerholes are located on the top side, and a further one or two beneath the snout. The flute could be made of wood, soft stone, whale tooth, gourd or even tree gum. Although sometimes blown forcefully as a whistle for signalling purposes, its main use was as a flute. *Nguru* scales are identical to normal *kōauau* scales, with additional notes for specimens with extra fingerholes beneath the snout. So, despite its different shape, the *nguru* may be considered a variety of *kōauau*. Because of the difficulty of construction, few if any *nguru* are still manufactured.

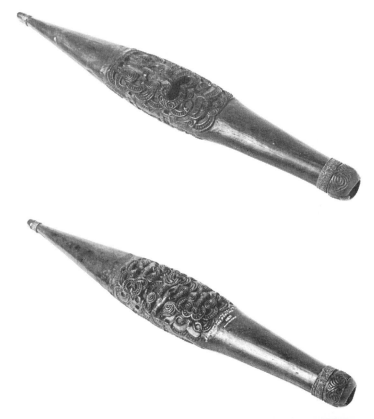

38. (Above) The front and rear of a heavily carved Maori *pūtōrino* bugle with a figure of eight sound hole. Length 520 mm (1 foot 8½ inches). (Auckland Museum. Copyright: University of Auckland.) (Below) Another heavily carved Maori *pūtōrino*, whose figure of eight sound hole is incorporated as the mouth of the face mask. Length 519 mm (1 foot 8 inches). (Copyright: National Museum of New Zealand, Wellington.)

39. A relatively small Maori *pūkāea* trumpet bound with flax. Length 750 mm (2 feet 5½ inches). (Auckland Museum. Copyright: University of Auckland.)

End-blown bugle

Like the larger war trumpet (see below), the Maori *pūtōrino* bugle is made by splitting lengthwise a piece of wood, hollowing it and binding it together again. There is a blowing hole at one end, a figure of eight sound hole in the centre, and a small hole at the other end (figure 38). Many specimens are heavily carved on both the front and back, and the sound hole is frequently incorporated into a face mask whose mouth is the hole itself. Although it is technically possible to blow small specimens as flutes, early accounts indicate that the *pūtōrino* was a trumpet and used for signalling rather than purely musical purposes. It is now obsolete.

War trumpet

Polynesia's only wooden trumpet is the New Zealand Maori *pūkāea* (figure 39). Now obsolete, the trumpet was sounded in single blasts by watchmen inside fortified villages in times of emergency. Its unusual construction technique is identical to that of another Maori instrument, the *pūtōrino* bugle (see above).

40. (Above) Two Hawaiian gourd flutes. Diameter of left-hand instrument 60 mm or 2½ inches). (Below) Two Tahitian gourd flutes. Diameter of left-hand instrument 43 mm or 1¾ inches). (Museum of Mankind, London. Copyright of both: Museum of Mankind.)

A straight branch up to 2 metres (6 feet) long is split lengthwise into several wedges, which are then hollowed and replaced; the bell is made separately from several sections of wood and is laced to the body of the instrument; the whole instrument is then bound together with flax or thin aerial roots. One end of the *pūkāea* has a wooden mouthpiece, and the overall shape of the instrument is conical, the other end flaring out to a bell. The concept of the instrument's sound being that of a human voice is such that some specimens have wooden protrusions in the bore near the bell, either carved there or inserted through the wall; these represent the human uvula or tonsils.

Gourd flutes

Globular flutes made from small gourds were used in Hawaii, New Zealand and Tahiti (figure 40). Despite their smallness (some are as little as 3 cm or 1¼ inches in diameter) they can accommodate a blowing hole (at the position where the stalk was removed) and up to three fingerholes and produce a series of loud and clear pitches. Hawaiian specimens were blown with the nose. Very little information is available on this kind of flute, which appears to have been used exclusively for personal entertainment. (A variant form occurred also in Hawaii, where perforated gourds were swung rapidly on a length of string to produce a loud whirring sound.)

4
Stringed instruments

Mouth-bow

Stringed instruments are rare in Polynesia. Although the musical bow has been reported from the Marquesas, its existence is well documented in Hawaii. The similarity between its Hawaiian name, *'ūkēkē*, and that of the Hawaiian jew's harp, *'ūkēkē hahau* ('struck musical bow'), reflects the fact that both instruments rely on the same principle of sound production using the mouth cavity to produce and vary the timbre. The Hawaiian bow was made of flat wood and required bridges at the end to keep the two or three strings clear of the frame. The strings, originally of twisted coconut fibre but more recently of horsehair or nylon gut, were first tuned by winding them around a fishtail-shaped projection at one end. Insertion of the bridges allowed final adjustments to pitch. Tunings are reported to have varied widely among instruments; one common pattern involved a combination of major second and perfect fourth above the lowest pitch (for example, G A D). Additional pitches were obtained by fingering individual strings during performance.

To play the bow, used as an aid to courting, the instrument was held horizontally to the left of the player's face, with the strung surface facing away from the face (figure 41). The right end of the instrument was held between the lips and individual strings were plucked by a plectrum held in the right hand. While the strings were plucked, the tongue and shape of the mouth changed, the player silently 'singing' his serenade. The combination of rhythmic and melodic patterns generated in this manner were reputedly intelligible to the loved one. Although common use of the bow during courting has now ceased, it is reported that the instrument is still occasionally played for private amusement.

Guitar

The history of the acoustic Spanish guitar in Polynesia is rather obscure. In the early nineteenth century the instrument was popular among both missionaries and the crews of whaling ships. The most widespread change occurring in Polynesia was the removal of one string, usually the lowest, and the retuning of the remaining five strings to an open major chord. This new tuning facilitated basic harmonic changes (they could now be barred with one finger) and made available several melodic patterns which developed into stereotypes. The instrument's portability and versatility have made it the standard form of accompaniment to popular solo and small-group songs, either on its own or in groups or together with other stringed instruments. Although tropical conditions are generally detrimental to stringed instruments, few if any attempts at preservation are made, and most specimens show clear signs of extensive use, such as worn lacquer and rusting steel strings.

The steel guitar developed in two separate and unique ways in Hawaii. The main feature of the so-called slack-key guitar is its tunings. The open strings usually include the pitches of a major triad, although the overall tuning is determined by the player. Many tunings exist, each appropriate to a particular melodic or harmonic sequence. Some tunings are given names and handed down as a kind of property within individual families. Slack-key style favours plucking over strumming and many pieces are based on constant repetitions of melodic or rhythmic patterns, and it is used for either solo or accompanying roles. There is evidence that certain dance-accompaniment rhythms typical of those for the Hawaiian skin and gourd drums have been incorporated into some slack-key compositions, thus giving an element of continuity to Hawaii's constantly evolving music.

The Hawaiian steel guitar, also called simply 'steel guitar', developed from an acoustic Spanish guitar laid on its back, a metal comb rather than the fingers pressed against the strings to change their pitch. Further developments included a steel bar replacing the comb, finger and thumb-picks on the plucking hand, new tunings, and later electrification, a reshaping to a more rectangular form, and incorporation in a stand complete with foot pedals to control overall loudness and also the pitch of each string. Performance may feature the use of wide vibrato, slides between notes or chords, and manipulation of the loudness or softness of individual notes. Having suffered a decline in interest in the 1930s, the steel guitar appears now to be enjoying a revival.

Ukulele

This instrument, now used throughout Polynesia and beyond, originated as a four-stringed Portuguese instrument called *bra-guinha*, which was introduced into Hawaii in 1879 by Portuguese immigrants. Its present name translates literally as 'jumping flea' and there are several versions of the origin of the term. Beginning

41. A model using a musical bow (*'ūkēkē*). (Copyright: Bishop Museum, Honolulu.)

as a provider of rhythmic backing for voices or other instruments, the ukulele's popularity spread rapidly, and popular solo compositions began in the 1920s. Later developments included tenor and baritone models and distinctive picking and strumming techniques. In Polynesian islands outside Hawaii the instrument maintains its original small size and several tunings are in current use. Although most specimens are imported, local variations may have a belly constructed from an empty can or coconut shells — the so-called 'cocolele'. And although there are a few outstanding soloists, the ukulele features most commonly as part of a string band, together with guitars and the occasional banjo or one-string bass.

5
Museums

Although many museums may contain a few Polynesian sound-producing instruments, those mentioned below have collections which are comprehensive.

Great Britain
Cambridge University Museum of Archaeology and Anthropology, Downing Street, Cambridge CB2 3DZ. Telephone: 0223 337733 or 333516.

Museum of Mankind (Ethnography Department of the British Museum), 6 Burlington Gardens, London W1X 2EX. Telephone: 071-323 8043.

New Zealand
Auckland Institute and Museum, Auckland Domain, Auckland 1.

United States of America
American Museum of Natural History, 79th Street and Central Park West, New York, NY 10024.

Bishop Museum, 1525 Bernice Street, Honolulu, Hawaii 96817.

Peabody Museum of Salem, 161 Essex Street, Salem, Massachusetts 01970.

Smithsonian Institution, 1000 Jefferson Drive SW, Washington DC 20560.

62

6
Further reading

Collaer, Paul. *Musikgeschichte in Bildern: Ozeanien*. Deutcher Verlag für Musik, Leipzig, 1965.

Fischer, Hans. *Sound-Producing Instruments in Oceania*. Institute of Papua New Guinea Studies, Boroko, 1983.

Kanahele, George (editor). *Hawaiian Music and Musicians; An Illustrated History*. University Press of Hawaii, Honolulu, 1979.

Moyle, Richard M. *Tongan Music*. Auckland University Press, Auckland, 1987.

Moyle, Richard M. *Traditional Samoan Music*. Auckland University Press, Auckland, 1988.

Moyle, Richard M. *The Sounds of Oceania*. Auckland Museum, Auckland, 1989.

Sadie, Stanley (editor). *The New Grove Dictionary of Musical Instruments* (three volumes). Macmillan, London, 1984. Useful articles can be found on musical instruments under their local names, as well as under their English counterparts.

Index

Page numbers in italic refer to illustrations